I0726565

REGNUM IN POTENTIA

Saturn's Kingdom Transformed Into The Golden Age

By Tracy R. Twyman

Quintessential Publications
(2011)

quintessentialpublications.com

ISBN: 978-1-962312-23-3

Table of Contents

Part I: Saturn's Kingdom Transformed Into the Golden Age

Part I: Saturn's Kingdom Transformed Into the Golden Age

As I join the world in watching with awe the revolutions unfolding throughout the Middle East, and the spirited revolt that seems to be spreading across the West, I can't help but think that we are really witnessing the dawning of a new era. The revolution that is spreading is spearheaded largely by the disenfranchised youth of the world. Educated and hard-working but unable to obtain a job, feed themselves, or raise a family, and with no future prospects whatsoever, the present generation has no choice but to fight for survival. Moreover, the elder generation of ruling class, grown fat on the blood of their subjects and dependant on their servants for everything, have laid upon this generation an enormous, unpayable debt burden that has been built up over the last several generations, and demanded that the youth of today now pay the full price for the sins — the laziness, selfishness, and neglect — practiced by their forefathers. Not surprisingly, the answer to this call has been a resounding "Hell no." The elite, who weren't expecting such an insolent reaction, are now attempting to bomb, shoot, and bludgeon their young slaves into submission. It won't work. We have reached the nadir of a historically repeating cycle. This is a moment born of destiny.

Whitney Houston sang "I believe the children are the future," but throughout history, the prevailing attitude has been that the sacrifice of the future of children, and the children of the future, is the predominant source of sustenance for the present population. Indeed, as I point out in my book *Money Grows on the Tree of Knowledge*, our own civilization has been built around the concept of stealing the wealth of the future, in order to manufacture artificial wealth to be enjoyed by ruling class adults in the present. In this book, I demonstrate that this is analogous to the story in Greek mythology of Chronos eating his own children to eliminate rivals and assure the continuance of his rule.

In alchemical studies, this myth is used as a metaphor for the production of gold from lead. In the book I demonstrate how the entire economy is built around alchemical processes, and that the central mystery of alchemy is child sacrifice. The alchemical process is a metaphorical formula for transformation that can be applied to all manner of different things. This includes the turning of the ages: the evolution of man, both physically and spiritually, through the passage of lengthy aeons of time.

Saturn with his scythe, leaning on a cane

In that book I talked about the concept that the Greeks and Romans had of the Golden Age. Their poets wrote of a four-step cycle of aeons that life on Earth went through repeatedly. Each age was named after a metal, and each was considered a devolution from the previous era. Some Roman writers said that the races which ruled each era were actually made of these metals. Sometimes these are said to be different races of "men," although the accounts make it clear that the earlier races were not ordinary men, but gods, and the later races were the hybrid children of gods mating with humans.

The race of the Heroic Era (from which Hercules, Jason and Odysseus came) was such a hybrid race. Sometimes a fifth age was added, that of Stone, said to be the present age. The men of the present age were said to have been produced when the heroes of the Greek Deluge myth, Deucalion and Pyrrha, washed up in their Ark on Mount Parnassus. Allegedly, they pulled a cloth over their heads to blindfold them, and then threw stones behind their backs, which magically turned into human children, our ancestors. Ours is said to be a devolved version of the race of heroes, the divine DNA of our forefathers watered down with too much human blood.

Deucalion and Pyrrha creating the Stone Race after the Flood

However, what they all seem to agree on is that first was the Golden Age, in which, allegedly, the Earth was peopled by Gods, and Chronos (Saturn) was chief among them. But strangely, although he was Lord of the Earth, this was seen not as a time of autocratic rule, but peaceful anarchy. Saturn was thought of as the Lord of Unrule, and during this epoch, his subjects wanted for nothing. There was no money, nobody had to work for a living, and all things were held in common. It was a paradise in which everyone was free to do as they wished because there no lack, and therefore no need for involuntary compulsion through violent force. Or so it is implied.

Because of this, Saturn was associated with the Liberty Cap (also known as the Phrygian gap), a soft red floppy hat like Santa Claus wears (without the fuzzy cotton ball at the end). In the Roman empire, the Liberty Cap was worn by slaves who had been set free, either temporarily or permanently. When the Romans celebrated his festival at the end of the year (Saturnalia), no work was done, public drunkenness was encouraged, rules against gambling and prostitution were temporarily suspended, and slaves were given furloughs from their duties, let to run about as free men, with the red cap of liberty on their heads. A temporary sovereign was elected to represent the Lord of Misrule, who would eat and drink like a king until New Year's Day. He would give out gifts to children, and receive many gifts himself. In the earliest times in which this festival was observed, this king would "reign" (ritually) for a year, then be sacrificed at the end of next year's Saturnalia. In Plutarch's Lives, we read:

> "The Saturnalia was a feast celebrated on the 14th of the kalends of January Betide the sacrifices in honour of Saturn who upon his retiring into Italy introduced there the happiness of the golden age. Servants were at this time indulged in mirth and freedom in memory of the equality which prevailed in that age. Presents were sent from one friend to another and no war was to be proclaimed or offender executed It is uncertain when this festival was instituted."

Illustration from Goltzius based on Ovid's description of the Golden Age

Many aspects of these rites have survived into modern times. There are obvious parallels with our Christmas and New Year's celebrations, as I discussed in *Money Grows on the Tree of Knowledge*. The character of Saturn or the Lord of Misrule is obviously now played by Santa Claus. During the season, children stay home from school and most people take significant time off work. They drink, overeat, and kill each other stampeding in competition for the opportunity to purchase toys (and not always to give to children). As I discuss in that book, the alchemically-designed economy is built to be dependant upon this annual display of excess consumption to fuel the financial machine for the coming year.

Saturn riding in his chariot

The New Year celebrations, with their drunken orgies, definitely stem from Saturnalian origins as well. This is proven also by the symbolism used in modern times to depict New Year's time, with Father Time representing the old year and the New Year's Babe representing the coming annum. We make "New Year's resolutions" and sing "should auld acquaintance be forgot," just as our ancestors used this time to wash their hands of their past sins by laying them instead on the heads of a sacrificial victim. This role was played by Chronos and Dionysus in ancient times, with the latter being referred to as the "Child in the Harvest Basket" — the basket in which the sun god was said to make his annual voyage through the heavens This is also the traditional time at which the birth of Chronos' patricidal son Zeus was celebrated, "born at midwinter when the Sun entered the house of Capricorn" the goat, according to Robert Graves.

But there are other examples as well of the continuing celebration of Saturnalia. There is Childermass on December 26th, discussed in a previous article of mine, on which the Massacre of the Innocents is observed — a story linked by European alchemists specifically with the Greek story of Chronos eating his children. Then there is the Feast of the Epiphany on January 6th, and the related celebration of Mardi Gras which begins with that feast. This is the day on which the "festival of the manifestation of Christ to the Gentiles" is celebrated, and is traditionally the day on which the three magi came to the bedside of the baby Jesus bearing gifts.

Santa Claus riding a goat, representative of Capricorn, the sign that rules the time of Saturnalia, with a child in a basket tucked under his arm.

On this day it is customary to bake "epiphany cakes" (or "king cakes", as they are called in New Orleans), into which a tiny bean or token has been buried, representing the Christ child. Often it is an actual plastic baby. Sometimes the cake itself is also made out of marzipan and formed into the shape of a baby. Each guest at an Epiphany party will get their own cake, but only one of them, chosen at random, will contain the baby token. Whichever guest gets the baby served to them is the

"King" of the party, and will be treated to special party favors. (They literally shout "I've got the baby!" to everyone in the room when the token is discovered.)

The downside, however, to being chosen is that the King has to clean up the mess at the end, or is responsible for hosting the party next year. The parallels to King Saturn eating his children, and the practice at Saturnalia of a temporary king being chosen for sacrifice, are obvious. So too are the connections between Saturnalia and Carnival, which is celebrated in New Orleans from January 6th until Ash Wednesday in March, when we begin to celebrate Christ's sacrifice on the cross. These traditions all date back to the 18th century. But it is said that the sacrificial king of the Roman Saturnalia was chosen in a similar fashion. The implication hidden in the rite is that the king chosen by lot is the one who eats the baby, just as Saturn did, but in so doing he seals the fate of his own doom. The fact that in Europe a sabot (a device used in firearms) was used for the token in the cake makes the implied threat even more obvious.

Another similar modern-day celebration is that of Vasilopita on New Year's Day in the Balkans and Eastern Europe. The word literally means "King Pie," although the holiday has in modern times been associated with St. Basil, who's feast day is celebrated on that date also. There are many different versions of his story, but they all involve distributing cakes amongst the townspeople in which coins of various values were hidden at random. "Basil" means "king" in old French and Greek, so the choosing of this Saint to represent this day and this ritual cannot be a coincidence. The date is celebrated much like the Feast of the Epiphany, with a coin being the traditional token in the cake.

The details of the rite are rather interesting. A single cake is used, cut into slices, with one of them containing the cake. The cutting of the cake takes place at midnight on New Year's Eve and involves everyone in the household. The sign of the cross is etched onto the top, and then slices are given out to everyone, the eldest receiving theirs first. It is also traditional to slice a piece to sacrifice to the Kallikantzaroi. They are described as having hairy bodies, hooves for feet, and sporting enormous erect penises, like tradition satyrs in Greek mythology. The name is said to mean "beautiful centaur," named after the legendary creatures described as horses from the waist down but with the heads of men.

The Kallikantzaroi were believed to live underground at the center of the Earth, at the bottom of the World Tree, in Greek tradition. This is

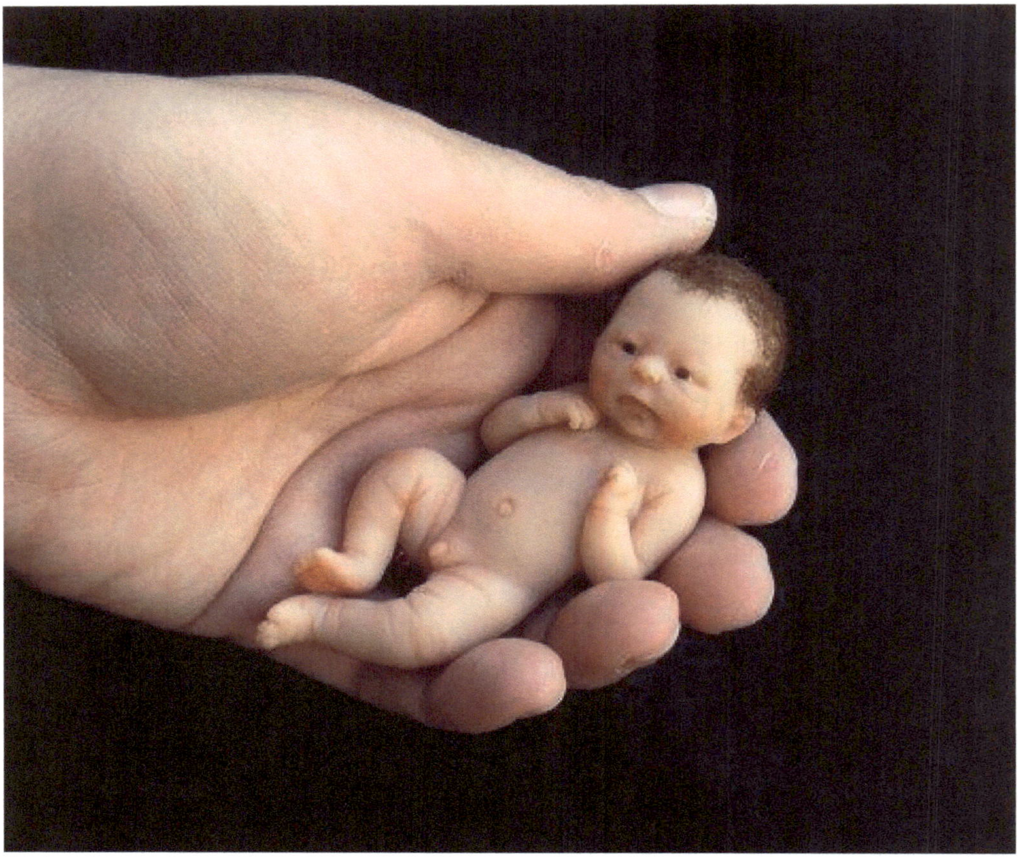

A marzipan Epiphany cake in the shape of a baby

Mardi Gras king cake with plastic baby token

described as being a pole that holds the heavens apart from the Earth. These demons are said to be constantly trying to saw down the trunk of the tree so that it will collapse. But just as they are about to succeed each year, tradition states that on Christmas day, the sun "stops moving" temporarily. The Kallikantzaroi are released from their underground prison and come to the surface to torment human beings, which they do until the 6th of January. Then, on the Feast Day of the Epiphany, the sun is said to start moving again, and the demons become trapped underground once more. There they find that all of their work sawing the World Tree has been undone, and they must start over again.

So here we have a few interesting connections. For one thing, this information confirms my speculation in an earlier article that the tradition of leaving cookies for Santa Claus might be reminiscent of an older folk tradition in which food sacrifices were laid out to satisfy the Saturnian child-eating entity represented by Santa Claus, in hopes that he doesn't eat the children instead. Indeed, the concept of a token representing a baby is being hidden inside of a cake specifically brings to mind the subterfuge of Rhea, Chronos' wife, who substituted a stone for the baby Zeus when Chronos came to devour him as a newborn infant. Secondly, we have a connection between these bizarre Saturnian rituals at Christmas and the concept of global cataclysm, specifically the destruction of the Earth's present polar configuration. I will get into this in more detail later on.

The alchemist Fulcanelli wrote in *The Mystery of the Cathedrals* about the connections between the Epiphany Day rituals and the symbolism of alchemy. The child in the cake stands for the gold hidden within the lead (represented by Saturn), which must be divulged and refined through the alchemical process, like a soul being extracted from a human body. He writes:

> "As for the common subject of the Work, some call it Magnesia lunarii; others, who are more sincere, call it Lead of the Wise, vegetable Saturn. Philalethes, Basil Valentine and the Cosmopolite say Son or Child of Saturn. ....Therefore, brothers, if you pay attention to what I have said about the Epiphany cake (galette des Rois)... you will no longer have any doubt about the subject which you must choose; its common name will be clearly known to you. You will then be in possession of this Chaos of the Wise 'in which all hidden secrets exist in potential', as Philalethes asserts, and which the skilled artist will not hesitate to actualize. Open, that is to say decompose, this matter.

The World Tree, where the Kallikantzaroi do their evil deeds
From *Northern Antiquities*, an English translation of the Prose Edda from 1847. Painted by Oluf Olufsen Bagge.

An ancient celebration of the Saturnalia.

> Try to separate the pure part of it, or its metallic soul as the sacred expression has it, and you will have the kirmis, the Hermes, the mercury dye which has within it the mystic gold, just as St. Christopher carries Jesus and the ram carries its own fleece. You will understand why the Golden Fleece is hung on the oak, like the gall and the kirmis, and you will be able to say, without violating the truth, that the old hermetic oak acts as mother to the secret mercury. By comparing legends and symbols, light will dawn in your mind and you will know the close affinity which unites the oak to the ram, St. Christopher to the Child-King, the Good Shepherd to the lamb, the Christian counterpart of Hermes Criophorus (the ram bearer), etc."

Later on, Fulcanelli describes an image inside a cathedral involving a dragon which he says is, in code, depicted as using its flaming breath to cook a child inside of an athanor. This child is said to be a king, and the son of the dragon himself, through the rape of a human female, a princess. He says:

> "This monstrous beast, with the grace of some great lizard, used to embrace the athenor, leaving in its flames the triply-crowned little king, who is the son of its violent acts on the dead adultress. Only the face of the mineral child appears as it undergoes the 'baths of fire' mentioned by Nicholas Flamel. It is here swathed and tied up like the figure of the little 'bather,' still found today in Epiphany cakes."

Fulcanelli says that the child Mercury, the Philosopher's Stone, shut up in the prison of the athanor, is like the baby imprisoned within the epiphany cake:

> "Even the very pastry of the cake obeys the laws of traditional symbology. This pastry is flaky and our little bather is shut up in it like a book marker. This is an interesting confirmation of the matter represented by the Epiphany cake. Sendivogius tells us that the prepared mercury has the aspect and form of a stony mass, crumbly and flaky. 'If you look at it closely,' he says, 'you will notice that it is all flaky.' Indeed, the crystalline layers, which form this substance, lie one above the other like the leaves of a book...."

He then goes on to say:

> "The popular expression to take the cake means to be fortunate. The one who is fortunate enough to find the bean in the cake has no further need for anything; he will never lack money. He will be doubly king, by science and by fortune."

So the message is that the fortunate one is the one who eats the baby, because he gets to be king. But his luck is soon to run out, because as we know, at the very earliest roots of this ritual, it is the king who pays the price at next year's Saturnalia rite. This is the central mystery upon which all of our social institutions are based. This pattern can be found within society in numerous ways, and can even be measured over the course of vast aeons of time.

As I stated in *Money Grows on the Tree of Knowledge*, there is a moral dilemma implied in the story of Chronos/Saturn. Saturn is associated with liberty, and a Golden Age of peaceful anarchy. Yet we know that in order to maintain this form of rule, he killed his own children to prevent them from growing up to overtake him. The only reason the Golden Age was so golden was because Saturn's children were paying the price of the sacrifice.

THE KING OF THE BEAN.

Drawing depicting the Feast of the Epiphany with king cake ritual.

But this is par for the course. Chronos himself had overthrown his father Ouranos, castrated him and imprisoned him in the depths of the Earth. Chronos too had narrowly escaped death as a child, since his father had also tried to kill all of his children at birth, for the same reason. In some versions of the myth, Ouranos tried to keep them from being born by imprisoning them within the mother's womb.) Since their mother was Gaia (Earth), this meant that they were shut up in Tartarus, the lowest chamber of the underworld, called "the prison of the Sons of Earth," this is also where the Titans were jailed by Zeus after he overthrew them.

Here is the meaning of this myth. Chronos ("Father Time") had lived and ruled (or "unruled) for untold aeons in a timeless realm before the coming of Zeus. In this realm, there could be no begetting of offspring, or else there would also be death. Thus the birth of children had to be prevented, either by confining them within the womb — as Ouranos did — or by swallowing them at birth — as Chronos did, attempting to negate their existence by confining them to another womb of sorts: his gullet.

Chronos castrating Uranus.

This is exactly what the story of the Garden of Eden indicates. Adam and Eve live in happy, timeless ignorance. They are the children of a god who remains, to them, invisible, and they are still shut up inside the womb, or within their father's gullet. There, they live as parasites, forming a symbiotic relationship with their host, who provides them with all of the sustenance they need. Then one day, a foreign fruit is introduced to them from outside. They are told by their father, the unseen god, not to eat it. But they do anyway, and it initiates in them an awakening to the reality of what they are involved in. Their eyes are opened. They wake up from the dream and realize that they are slowly being digested. At that moment, they are vomited out into the cold, cruel, outside world, forced to work for their daily bread, fighting for survival. With their birth, or perhaps, their second birth, the passage of time is finally allowed to begin.

As we read of the passages of the various ages, from Golden to Silver, then to Bronze, Iron and (some say) Stone, we understand that the transition from one aeon to the next is always marked by a revolution of a similar sort, in which the disenfranchised son of the king, the rightful

The mutilation of Uranus by Saturn

inheritor to the throne, escapes death and overtakes his tyrant father. If the father is a divine god-king (as in the oldest myths), he doesn't really die, but instead falls into a death-like sleep and is imprisoned in the center of the Earth. There he waits to be avenged and reincarnated in a new king, reigning over a new age.

Another depiction of the Golden Age

What these myths of the Golden Age, Garden of Eden, and other primordial paradises really point to is the concept of a cosmic center: a kingdom that doesn't really exist, except in the Otherworld, in potentia. But it is said to be at the heart of our own existence, and its essence can be felt everywhere. It is a place where there is no time as we know it. Rather, all points of time exist simultaneously, and all space as well. This is why the people who live there are said to never grow old. Presently, in our own time, we perceive it as fallen, like Eden, Atlantis, or the sunken R'lyeh of H.P. Lovercraft's stories. But the legends state that that there will come a time in the future when a new age will dawn, and the hidden, sunken kingdom will rise again, the old king reborn to rule again, instantly transforming our own mundane world into the timeless paradise formerly relegated to the Otherworld.

This is exactly how the relationship between Osiris and Horus was viewed by the Egyptians. There was never a time when Osiris was really alive ruling his kingdom on Earth. From the earliest times he was thought to be in the center of the Earth, in his tomb at the center of the World Mountain. His son Horus ruled on the surface as his reincarnation. But it was the existence of the undead Osiris in the underworld that gave Horus' throne its legitimacy.

This is also how the realm of the Fisher King is described in the Grail romances, who, like Ouranos, has been castrated, and now rules over a kingdom out of time. He can never die, but isn't really alive. Only the food from the Grail keeps him alive in this in-between state. His wound will never heal, but continually festers, and grows worse whenever Saturn is ascendant in the heavens.

We also find hints in the romances that the food of the Grail, which keeps the king alive and the rest of his subjects in perpetual youth, is in fact the flesh and blood of children. That this is what the "Elixir of Life" is made from is hinted at also in the alchemical texts of Europe, and in many myths from throughout the world. I explore these ideas at length in *Money Grows on the Tree of Knowledge*. This is the fruit of the Tree of Life that the gods of Genesis sought to prevent man from obtaining, lest we "live forever."

In Wolfram von Eschenbach's *Parzival*, the knight Gawain is sent on a mission by a hermit who looks young, although he is 75 years old. The mission is to find the sword that John the Baptist was beheaded with, which he will need to enter the lands of the Fisher King. The sword belongs to a pagan king named Gurguran, who promises Gawain that he can have it if he will rescue the king's son from a giant who has kidnapped him. Gawain kills the giant, but the boy is strangled to death in the process. Then, in a strange rite, Gurguran chops his sons body into pieces and distributes them to his subjects to eat. Gawain then receives the sword and is led to the Grail banquet at the Fisher King's court, where 12 knights who are hundreds of years old (reminiscent of the 12 Olympian gods) sit around a banquet hall, all looking youthful except for their grey hair.

The reason why the hidden kingdom always exists, but never really, except in potentia, is because it is the place where time began. Yet if there is no time, how can there be a beginning? Therefore through paradox and logical fallacy it negates its own existence. Such is the case with the land of Nod, the wilderness land where Cain was exiled to, and where he built his kingdom. His descendants shared the same names as those of his brother Seth, save for a single letter, indicating their non-being. The chronology of their birth is slightly different than that of Seth's descendants because time has no meaning where they are.

The Golden Age, with Saturn or Chronos shown flying overhead in his chariot, eating a baby.
Beham oder Pencz-*Die sieben Planeten-Venus-Sonn*-1531

Cain, like Saturn, lived in perpetual fear of being killed by one of his descendants in revenge, as it had been prophesied, according to tales recounted in Louis Ginzberg's book Legends of the Jews. Thus in Genesis Cain cries out to God in lamentation that he must forever remain in hiding, a "fugitive and a vagabond," because "Whosoever findeth me shall slay me." This eventually transpired when he was killed by his descendant Lamech in a hunting accident, since Cain's horns, given to him by God supposedly as a protective mark to keep him safe from murder, caused him to be mistaken for an animal and shot — yet another dirty trick from Jehovah. Then, having killed his own ancestor, while hunting in the wilderness of the timelessness of Nod, Lamech, and all of Cain's descendants, ceased to be, or to have ever been. From that moment on the Bible acknowledges them no more.

This is exactly how Edith Hamilton summarizes Homer's description of the underworld of the dead, Hades, in his epic The Odyssey, according to her classic book Mythology: Timeless Tales of Gods and Heroes, where she wrote:

> In Homer the underworld is vague, a shadowy place inhabited by shadows. Nothing is real there. The ghosts' existence, if it can be called that, is like a miserable dream.

But the underworld is just part of this nebulous realm of the gods, which is clearly separate from our own world, and yet accessible from certain parts of our world, and in some ways strangely entangled with it. This larger divine realm came to be termed "Olympus" by the Greeks, but the exact meaning of this term is hard to specify. As Edith Hamilton explains:

> "The twelve great Olympians were supreme among the gods who succeeded the Titans. They were called the Olympians because Olympus was their home. What Olympus was, however, is not easy to say. There is no doubt that at first it was held to be a mountain top, and generally identified with Greece's highest mountain, Mt. Olympus in Thessaly, in the northeast of Greece. But even in the earliest Greek poem, the Illiad, this idea is beginning to give way to the idea of an Olympus in some mysterious region far above all the mountains of the earth. In one passage of the Illiad Zeus talks to the gods from "the topmost peak of many-ridged Olympus," clearly a mountain. Even so, it is not heaven. Homer makes Poseidon say that he rules the sea, Hades the dead, Zeus the heavens, but Olympus is common to all three."

These are details common to just about any description of the popular motif of the World-Mountain, found in almost every culture around the globe. It is the location of the World Tree, and the pole that holds the heavens aloft from the Earth. The depths of the mountain's caverns and the roots of the tree reach down into the lowest level of existence, while the top of the mountain, and the top of the tree, reaches the highest level of heaven in existence. Summarizing this entire body of legends from around the world, Julius Evola wrote in *The Mystery of the Grail*:

> "These are first and foremost symbols of centrality: the center, the pole, the region in the middle of the earth, the central stone or the foundation, the magnet. Then, symbols of stability: the island surrounded by the waters, the rock, the unshakable stone. Finally, symbols of inviolability and inaccessibility; the invisible or not-to-be-found castle or land, a wild mountain peak, a subterranean region. Moreover, the 'Land of Light,' the 'Land of the Living,' the 'Holy Land.' Yet again, all the variations of the golden symbolism, which, on the one hand, includes all the notions of solarity, light, regality, immortality, and incorruptibility while, on the other hand, it has always had some relationship with the primordial tradition and with the age characterized by gold. Other symbols point to 'life' in the higher sense of the word (e.g., the 'perennial food'; the 'Tree of Life'), to a transcendent knowledge, to an invincible power; everything appears variously mixed in the fantastic, symbolic, or poetic representations that in the various traditions have foreshadowed this constant theme of the invisible regnum and of the Supreme Center of the world, in itself or in its emanations and reproductions."

But according to several different researchers specializing in several different fields, long before, and long after, the Titanic Golden Age was conquered by Zeus, and the cosmic pole renamed Olympus, the ancients thought of the magical realm of World-Mountain as being associated with Saturn. As Joscelyn Godwin writes in *Arktos: The Polar Myth*:

> "Ancient Iranian astronomers identified the pole as 'Saturn's womb,' and so did the neoplatonists of Greece."

Julius Evola concurs, writing of the kingdom at the pole that:

> "Moreover, according to a classical tradition, after having been the lord of this earth, the king of the Golden Age, Kronos-

The Grail castle as the hidden kingdom at the center of the universe.

> Saturn, was dethroned and castrated (that is, deprived of the power to beget, to give life to a new stock); he still lives, though asleep, in a region located in the Far North, close to the Arctic Sea, which was also called the Cronid Sea."

Castle of the Grail by Ferdinand Knab

Here we touch upon what is perhaps the most mind-blowing concept hinted at in this whole collection of myths that we are presently examining. Saturn's kingdom, because it's timeless, is still there, enclosed within a prison of timelessness, surrounded by space-time. His death-like sleep is, in fact, the prison itself, for as Plutarch writes, "his slumber had been artfully produced in order to chain him, and round about him were many dæmons for his guards and servants." His dreams are the shackles which bind him. Like the blissfully ignorant children of the Garden of Eden, he is bound in a hypnotic state by his own illusions. He has switched places with those he devoured. Plutarch writes about Saturn's hidden kingdom of dreams, which he describes as being on an island, in his *Morals*. I find it worthy of lengthy quotation.

"... the barbarians fable that Saturn is imprisoned by Jupiter, whilst his son lies by his side, as though keeping guard over those islands and the sea, which they call 'the Sea of Saturn.' ... That sea-coast of the mainland Greeks are settled on, around a bay not smaller than the Mæotis, the entrance of which lies almost in a straight line opposite the entrance to the Caspian Sea. Those Greeks call and consider themselves continental people, but islanders all such as inhabit this land of ours, inasmuch as it is surrounded on all sides by the sea; and they believe that with the peoples of Saturn were united, later, those who wandered about with Hercules, and being left behind there, they rekindled into strength and numbers the Greek element, then on the point of extinction, and sinking into the barbarian language, manners, and laws; whence Hercules has the first honours there, and Saturn the second."

Illustration from the New Atlantis

Plutarch then goes on to describe a strange sacrificial rite in which the "servants of Saturn" are sent out on perilous voyages to this island, where they serve him for a period of thirteen years, after which they have the choice of staying in his realm or returning home. However, it is unclear in what capacity they "serve," since Saturn's is a realm of "abundance without toil and trouble." It seems to be more of a philosophical academy, akin to the "Philosophic Kingdom" of Sir Francis Bacon's *New Atlantis*. Interestingly, in that book Bacon used an illustration of Saturn unveiling the naked Lady Venus in her secret tomb in the Venusberg (a mythical mountain almost identical in description to Saturn's island). This is a Hermetic symbol of the unveiling of the secrets of nature through alchemy, and it is said that whoever unveils Venus is cursed to remain a prisoner in her underworld kingdom forever within the caverns of her enchanted mountain at the center of the Earth, where she rests in a death-like sleep, "vivit- non vivit," just like Saturn.

On Saturn's island, the god teaches them by communicating through apparitions and dreams. That's also how he keeps them on the island. He keeps them in a state of enchantment, just as Venus is said to do to the young men who visit her secret realm. As Plutarch describes it:

> "But when the star of Saturn, which we call the 'Informer,' but they 'Nocturnal,' comes into the sign of the Bull every thirty years, they having got ready a long while beforehand all things required for the sacrifice and the games … they send out people appointed by lot in the same number of ships, furnished with provisions and stores necessary for persons intending to cross so vast a sea by dint of rowing, as well as to live a long time in a foreign land. When they have put to sea, they meet, naturally, with different fates, but those who escape from the sea, first of all, touch at the foremost isles, which are inhabited by Greeks also, and see the sun setting for less than one hour for thirty days in succession; and this interval is night, attended with slight darkness, and a twilight glimmering out of the west. Having spent ninety days there, treated with honour and hospitality, being both considered and entitled 'holy,' thenceforward they voyage with the help of the winds. No other people inhabit the islands save themselves and those that had been sent out before; it is, indeed, allowed to such as have served thirteen years in waiting upon the god, to return home, but the greatest part prefer to remain there, partly out of habit, partly because they have all things in abundance without toil

> and trouble, as they pass their time in sacrifices and hymn singing, or in studying legends and philosophy of some sort. For wonderful are both the island and the mildness of the climate; whilst the deity himself has been an obstacle to some when contemplating departure, by manifesting himself to them as to familiars and friends, not by way of dreams or by tokens, but conversing with them in a visible form with many apparitions and speeches of genii. For Saturn himself is imprisoned in a vast cavern, sleeping upon a rock overlaid with gold; for his sleep has been contrived by Jupiter for his chaining—whilst birds fly down from the rock, which are ordained to carry ambrosia to him, whilst the island is overspread with fragrance, diffused from the rock as from a fountain. Those genii wait upon and nurse Saturn, who had been his companions at the time when truly he used to reign over both gods and men; and they, being endowed with prophecy, foretell, on their own account, many things, but important matters, and such as concern the highest things, they go down into the cavern and report as the dreams of Saturn; for whatsoever things Jupiter is devising for the future, Saturn dreams what they are about, and that which is kingly and divine. The stranger having been carried there, as he told us, and waiting upon the god at his leisure, he gained acquaintance with astrology and geometry as far as it is possible to advance, whilst he took up 'natural science' for his department of philosophy."

This is the "Invisible College" that the Rosicrucians wrote about. It is the Scholomance of Dracula, which (the story goes) 13 specially-chosen students would attend each year to learn magick from the Master himself, but only one would graduate and be permitted to "ride the Dragon." This is the same as the Devil's school that witches attend when they go to the Sabbath, when they rise the broomstick or the goat, just as Jason rode the Golden Ram to safety. So too did Mohammed ride the woman-horse Barak on the Night Journey to the "furthest mosque," after falling asleep on the magical pillow-stone that fell from Heaven, which was the foundation-stone of the world, and which became the cornerstone of the Kaaba, the holy cube. So too did Jacob glimpse the ladder to Heaven in a dream, after sleeping on the stone of Bethel (the house of God), the royal betyl or "thunderstone" that was also said to have fallen to Earth from Heaven. This is the same as the alchemical "Magnet of the Wise," the metaphorical lodestone that guides initiates to the sacred island where the otherworld is located. Or rather, perhaps, we should consider that the Magnet attracts to the initiate the transcendental location he seeks to find. It brings the hidden kingdom to him, transforming the designated space that he happens to be standing into the sacred space of the Otherworld, where Saturn lies, dreaming. According to Julius Evola in The *Mystery of the Grail*:

> "We have seen that of all the places in which the tests of the Grail's knights occur, the 'Island' and the 'Castle' seem to be in the forefront. The journey to such places should essentially be regarded sub specie interiaritatis, that is, in terms of a shift of consciousness to a world that is usually precluded to human beings."

And:

> "In its polar character this kingdom is immobile. It does not get closer to various points in the flow of history; rather it is the flow of history, to which men and kingdoms get more or less close."

What we really have here is the concept of the sorcerer's magic circle, which is drawn on the floor in chalk when conjuring spirits. Of this there are two types. One is meant to contain demons within it, so that you can safely conjure one and talk to him without the possibility of him getting loose or harming you. Supposedly, the demons cannot step outside of a properly prepared magic circle. In this way, it can be thought of as a bottle for holding a genie, much like the Ark of the Covenant was a container for the spirit of God. The word "Ark" means "container," and is the root of a family of words in several different languages that mean "coffin," "prison," "boat," and "secret." This is what Saturn's island prison/tomb really is.

The other type can be thought of more as a traveling vessel. The magician places himself within the circle, and then he can safely travel to unseen astral realms without harming his mortal body. The universe around him is transformed, but he retains his own little bit of his home reality within the circle. In this sense it is similar to a magic carpet.

This, I think, is what Noah's Ark really was. It was a Hermetically-sealed vessel made of magic, that allowed Noah and the other passengers to be raised up into a higher dimension so that, while the world transformed around them (dissolving into the prima materia of chaos, the primeval ocean), they stayed safe within. When they exited the Ark, they were literally in a whole new world. This is how the hero

Depiction of the Invisible College as a contained vehicle.

in all of the global cataclysm myths from throughout the world makes it through the trial.

In the oldest version of the tale, from Mesopotamia, the Flood hero, Utnapishtim, was told of the impending deluge from spirits who spoke to him through the walls of his house. They then instructed him on how to turn his own house into a vessel, in the shape of a perfect cube. Similarly the Kingdom of God or "New Jerusalem" in St. John's *Revelation* is a flying city in the form of a perfect cube. This must certainly be connected to the "cubic stone" of the alchemists.

Utnapishtim in his Ark

In *Mystery of the Cathedrals*, Fulcanelli takes the last chapter to talk about alchemical concepts of the Apocalypse. He speaks of the destruction and regeneration of the world as though it were an alchemical transformation, in which humanity must die, be dissolved into chaos (like the Philosophic Mercury) and be reborn. This discussion is sparked by his analysis in that chapter of a strange monument called the "Cyclic cross of Hendaye," found in a church courtyard in Basque France, Fulcanelli writes in *Mystery of the Cathedrals* that:

> "Whatever its age, the Hendaye cross shows by the decoration of its pedestal that it is the strangest monument of primitive millenarism, the rarest symbolical translation of chiliasm, which I have ever met. It is known that this doctrine, first accepted and then refuted by Origen, St. Denis of Alexandria and St. Jerome although it had not been condemned by the Church, was part of the esoteric tradition of the ancient hermetic philosophy."

By rearranging the oddly-spaced letters of the message on the cross's stand — "O crux ave spes unica (Hail o cross, the only hope)" — he obtained the following, hidden message: "Il est ecrit que la vie se refugie en un seul espace" ("It is written that life takes refuge in a single space"). The meaning of this, says Fulcanelli, is that:

> "... a country exists, where death cannot reach man at the terrible time of the double cataclysm. As for the geographical location of this promised land, from which the elite will take part in the return of the golden age, it is up to us to find it. For the elite, the children of Elias, will be saved according to the word of Scripture, because their profound faith, their untiring perseverance in effort, will have earned for them the right to be promoted to the rank of disciples of the Christ-Light. They will bear his sign and will receive from him the mission of renewing for regenerated humanity the chain of tradition of the humanity which has disappeared."

Depiction of the Flood from the Metamorphoses of Ovid

So Fulcanelli believed that we really are heading towards an Apocalyptic event, and that messages predicting it are embedded in this monument. Moreover, he thought that alchemists and other "elite" would be able to decode the symbols left behind by the initiates of the past to figure out a special country or "space" where they will be safe from the cataclysm.

In the next installment of this series, we will talk about the possible connections between Saturn's hidden kingdom and catastrophic Earth changes in the distant past, as well as the future. We will get into concepts of how the calendar may have been different during the Golden Age, and how it may change again in the future due to dramatic alterations in Earth's magnetic field. We will talk about Saturn as the "Magnet of the Wise," and the idea of a "Black Sun" at the center of the Earth that was thought to be responsible for generating this mysterious force.

Later on in this essay series, we will examine the type of governance represented by Saturn. We will examine the historic role that this figure was believed to have played as one of the early conquerors and civilizers of the Italian peninsula. We will also talk about stories of the alleged lost kingdom of Atlantis, and the possible connections with Saturn's Golden Age kingdom. We will consider the conceptual relationship between our world and the hidden world, to see if we can shed any light on why our social institutions operate the way they do.

> "The place which seems the most solid is perhaps the most unstable. We have a tendency to forget that we live on a volcano, at the center of great forces of strength ... all is accomplished in accordance with well-determined cycles. A 'Navigator' guides the ark ['arche'] in the flood ... We do not subscribe to the conventional and erroneous astrology. The stars in themselves exert no influence. They are but reference points in space."
>
> – "Chyren," a.k.a. Pierre Plantard, from the magazine Circuit, 1959

Part II: Fishing for Men

Part II: Fishing for Men

> "Up to now it has been assumed that all our cognition must conform to the objects; but ... let us once try whether we do not get farther with the problems of metaphysics by assuming that the objects must conform to our cognition."
>
> — Immanuel Kant, Critique of Pure Reason

> "We're an empire now, and when we act, we create our own reality. And while you're studying that reality — judiciously, as you will — we'll act again, creating other new realities, which you can study too, and that's how things will sort out. We're history's actors . . . and you, all of you, will be left to just study what we do."
>
> — Anonymous senior aide to President George W. Bush, as quoted by Ron Suskind, New York Times, October 17, 2004

In the Grail story, the hero Parzival comes upon the Grail castle by accident. He is on a quest for something else entirely, or so he thinks, although that object varies according to the version of the tale in question. However, at some point in his adventures, he comes across an old man fishing in a boat. He asks the man where he might find lodging for the night, and is pointed to a nearby castle with a tall tower. Only later does he discover that the man he spoke to was the lord of the castle and the king of the surrounding lands.

This is the Grail king, the "Rich Fisher" who lives on the food provided magically by the Grail, and rules by virtue of the power that it gives him. But his kingdom is sick, as he himself is sick, from a wound inflicted during battle with another king, to whom he is related biologically. Both the king and his kingdom are kept in a death-like dream state by the power of the Grail, but they suffer constantly because the king cannot be healed from his wound, called "the Dolorous Stroke." The wound gets more painful when Saturn is ascendant in the heavens, and is said to be "in the thigh," a phrase thought by many mythographers to be a euphemism for castration.

If this is so it might link him to Ouranos, the god-king who was castrated and dethroned by his son Chronos (Saturn). However, there are also many figures in mythology, including the Greek blacksmith god Hephaestus and the biblical patriarch Jacob, who became incurably wounded in the thigh at some point during their lives. The potential connection with Ouranos, though, is interesting, since this god, whom the Chaldeans called Oannes, was depicted by them as a man who was half-fish.

The Dolorous Stroke

But none of the details of a holy myth are ever present by accident. There is a reason why Parzival is led to the Grail castle by a man in a fishing boat who turns out to be the king. That's because it was really Parzival he was fishing for.

Jesus told his apostles, speaking of their training as miracle-workers and evangels, that he would teach them to be "fishers of men." What is the real meaning of this phrase and why is Christianity associated with the symbol of the fish? It is commonly said that this Christian emblem, the Ichthys symbol, is the "sign of Jonah" which Jesus said was the only sign that his disciples would be given to rest their faith upon. Jonah, you will recall, was the prophet swallowed whole by a whale in the Old Testament. The whale is associated by cabbalists with the sea monster Leviathan, who, Jewish legends state, is destined to be cut up and served for dinner to the righteous in a eucharistic rite at the end of time, after the final judgment, as a way of exacting revenge for the swallowing of Jonah.

But really, the idea of "fishing for men" alludes to the concept of setting a trap, baiting someone and luring them in, where they will be

The Christian Ichthys fish symbol

Christ the Fisher King

captured, killed, and consumed. When the Fisher King is sitting out on his boat, waiting for someone like Parzival to come by so that he can encourage him to go to the Grail castle, he is playing the role of the Psychopompus. This is a label applied to Hermes the trickster god, who is both the initiator for adepts of alchemy, so too is he the guide of souls traveling to the Otherworld.

In these things, there is no contradiction. Initiation always involves being lured with false promises. The mysteries one seeks when one joins a mystical fraternity are never those which were initially sought after by the candidate. Indeed, the initiate may not have even known he was on a quest for enlightenment. He is going about his business one day, and something piques his interest. He pulls on a thread and follows it all the way to the center of the labyrinth. Most of the people who make it there are but sacrifices, meant to be eaten by the Minotaur. In ancient societies, luring the sacrificial victim, whether human or animal, to the place of death via an elaborate ruse was often a major part of the rite.

The intention of the Fisher King in luring Parzival to his castle is different depending on which version of the story is being read. But one common theme is that he needs Parzival to heal him from his wound. In some versions, this can be achieved by magic if Parzival will only ask of the king a certain question, usually, "What ails thee?" The Fisher King apologizes to Parzival upon meeting him because he cannot rise to greet him. He then waits for Parzival to ask him what is wrong. When the young knight doesn't pick up on the hint right away, he is cursed by the king's court for his failure to do what was expected of him.

This is the way that the Fisher King, the Lord of Unrule, exerted his subtle influence. This is what it means to "rule but not rule," as the magical line of the Frankish Merovingian kings were said to have done. According to some Eastern mystics and proto-Nazi German magical orders, this describes the rule of the "Lord of the Earth," an eternally sleeping being who they believed to reside in the center of the world. From there is was thought that he manipulated events on the surface world by subtly influencing his human adepts to do what he wanted, through visions, dreams, oracles, and magic spells.

The way in which Parzival was lured to the Grail castle is similar to how Alice is enticed down the rabbit hole in Lewis Carroll's Alice's Adventures in Wonderland. When she sees the white rabbit scurrying around, late for his appointment, she becomes curious about where he is going, and follows him down his hole, falling a seemingly infinite distance. (Similarly, a white salamander played a role in Joseph Smith's initiation, showing him the location of a magic hole where the golden tablets of Mormonism were buried.) As if it were not already clear that this world underground is in fact the Underworld, Alice makes it obvious that this is Saturn's kingdom when she asks:

> "What if I should fall right through the center of the Earth and end up on the other side, where everything is upside-down?"

The wounded Fisher King lies on his bed

When she finally reaches the bottom of the hole, Alice learns that in order to follow the rabbit into his lair, she must shrink in size so that she can fit through the door. This indicates the multidimensional nature of the Underworld, which could fit into a single mustard seed, or could be larger than the entire universe. Alice accomplishes her size change by consuming a magical cake that says "Eat me," and a bottle of magic potion that says "Drink me." This shows that the initiatory substance, the Philosopher's Stone, the Apple of Wisdom, is in fact a living intelligence that can be consumed to create transformations in the body.

In the story of *Alice's Adventures in Wonderland*, the rabbit is clearly playing the role of the Psychopompus, the Judas goat, who lures his prey to initiation through sacrifice via the land of the dead. The concept of fishing for men in this fashion, using subtlety and trickery, is represented in the sub-story of "The Walrus and the Carpenter" that

Alice finds a bottle that asks her to drink it

was told to Alice by Tweedledee and Tweedledum. This story seems at first take to be totally nonsensical, but it is actually a metaphor for how Alice herself got down the rabbit hole.

In the story, a walrus and a carpenter (clearly an allusion to Jesus) live in a land where the sun shines at night. For food, they fish for oysters by hypnotizing them with false promises, calling them to come out from their beds beneath the ocean. When they come to the surface they are swallowed up into the belly of the walrus, just as Alice herself had been swallowed up by Wonderland. When Alice spoke aloud the words "Eat me!" and "Drink me!" she was describing what was, in fact, already happening to her.

Perhaps, like Persephone eating the pomegranate seeds offered to her by her captor, Hades, it was Alice's consumption of these itemsthat obliged her to remain for a spell in the Underworld (a common theme also in Jewish folk tales about the underwater castle of Asmodeus, the king of demons). The earlier story she was told of the oysters being invited by the Walrus and the Carpenter to come to dinner with them, before realizing that the dinner was them, was but foreshadowing of Alice's invitation to join the tea party. They are both really a coded reference to the Grail service of the Parzival legend, at which, it is implied, the blood and flesh of children was served.

The Mad Hatter character is an alchemist. Hat-makers, like alchemists, were at one time at high risk of developing permanent brain damage as a result of breathing the vapors of the liquid mercury they used in their trade. Significantly, the Hatter's tea party is being held in celebration of the "unbirthday" of the attendees. The negation of birth is apparently held holy in the topsy-turvy world of Wonderland.

Here we see the mystical concept of preventing the birth of the king's heir by swallowing the newborn as it emerges from the womb, just as King Saturn did to his children. Thus, while they remained in his belly, they had still technically never been born, but were "unborn." This is what is meant by the rabbit who is perpetually "late," a euphemism for being dead. The fact that the rabbit's watch is said to be "two days slow" indicates that he and the other subjects of the kingdom may never have been born to begin with. So the "unbirthday" cake given to Alice at the party may be a metaphor for the epiphany cake or king cake discussed in the previous installment of this series, which itself was a representation of King Saturn eating his own children.

Alice is presented with an unbirthday cake

Returning to the story of the curious oysters, the meaning of this metaphor was not lost on the screenwriters of Alice, a modern adaptation of Lewis Carroll's classic made to air on the SyFy Channel. In this film, Wonderland is a parallel universe that Alice is lured to when her fiancé is kidnapped. There, the Queen of Hearts feeds off of the souls of humans, captured from our own world. They are lured into Wonderland, just like Alice, through the "man-fishing" process.

Once there, they are imprisoned in a 24-hour make-believe casino. Here they are kept in a trance state, perpetually winning every rigged game the casino has to offer. The good feelings generated by the sensation of winning are channeled from the bodies of the prisoners through a special vent in the floor, then magically turned into potions that the queen and her court feed off of like drugs. The people of Wonderland refer to their captive humans as "oysters" because of the "precious pearls within" — their souls.

The description of the Wonderland casino prison on this SyFy channel program from 2009 resembles remarkably a metaphor used by economist Max Keiser, starting around the same time, of the "casino gulag" to describe the global economy. In his view, everyone in the peasant class here on Earth is forced to speculate with their earnings on the stock and bond market in order to avoid losing wealth every time the government inflates the fiat currency by alchemically printing more money. Since, like a casino, the game is rigged by the banking cartel, who can front-run the market with high-frequency trading and are insured against losses with government bailouts, they keep the gambler slaves playing by hypnotizing them with the prospect of being the one-in-a-million lucky slave who gets to win the jackpot.

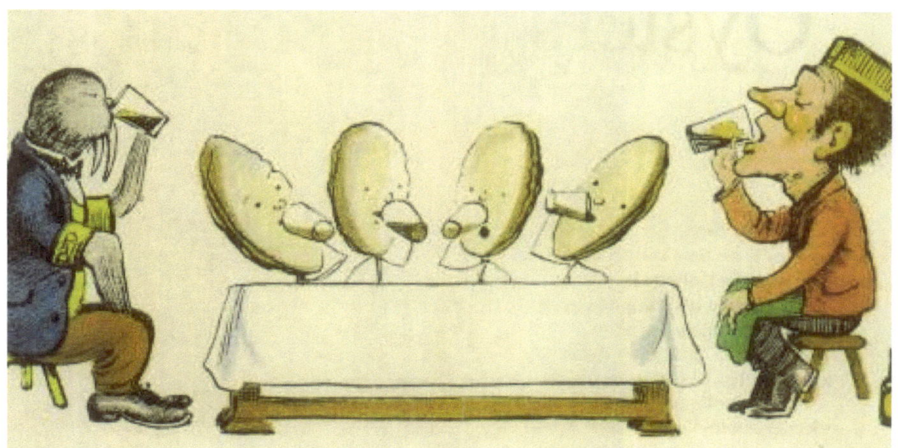

The Walrus and the Carpenter having drinks with the Curious Oysters

The people at the casino in *Alice* always win, or at least they feel like they do, and because of this, they are oblivious to the fact that they are prisoners. Towards the end, they are freed from their spell, and only when they stop playing the games do they remember the children that they have left abandoned at home. This is like the "Caucus Race" of the original Lewis Carroll story, a perfect metaphor for the modern rat race. At this event, people run around in a circle competing with each other, but with no end in mind, because "No one ever loses, and no one can ever win."

Another obvious comparison to be made with the casino gulag is, of course, to *The Matrix* film series. This story is replete with references to *Alice in Wonderland* from the very beginning, with the white rabbit playing the role of the initiator yet again (only this time waking the sleeping victim out of his dream state instead of luring him into it). The idea of human bodies being sucked of their essence by unseen monsters, their bodies used as batteries to power the machines of an unseen world, is in fact a perfect metaphor for our economy, and does correspond to many Gnostic descriptions of the universe.

The Walrus eating the Curious Oysters

So why do the monarchs of the hidden realm fish for men using subtlety instead of force? Well, for one thing, initiation must be freely sought by the initiate, like the Apple of Wisdom proffered by the serpent in Eden. Was it the intention all along that Adam and Eve would eat the forbidden fruit, obtain the forbidden knowledge, and fall down, down, down, like Alice, into another world? It seems likely.

The other thing is that, imprisoned as he is in the center of the Earth, lost eternally in a death-like slumber in the land of Nod — the land of Not! — there are not a lot of other options available to Saturn, the Lord of the Earth. Like Alice says, "When one is lost, it is best to wait for someone to find you." Just as Cain proclaimed "Whosoever findeth me shall slay me," Saturn passively awaits resurrection through the discovery of his tomb, as is the case with the sleeping occupants of the tombs of both Hermes and Christian Rosenkreutz.

The tomb of Venus, according to the Rosicrucian text *The Chemical Wedding of Christian Rosenkreutz*, is just like these other sacred tombs — in the center of the Earth, lit by an inner sun, etc. Guarding this tomb is a man who has been appointed this task since he accidentally stumbled on the naked body of Venus many centuries earlier. There he is, condemned to wait until someone else makes the same mistake and comes to take his place.

This like the story of Atlas, obliged to play the part of the World Tree, the Earth's mythical central pillar or pole, upholding the weight of the

Earth upon his back. There he must stay until someone else comes along that he can trick into taking his place (a role temporarily played by Hercules at one point). Likewise, Prometheus had to stay chained to Tartarus, having his liver eaten daily, until someone else agreed to be sacrificed in his stead (a role eventually played by Chiron).

On a similar note, in the New Testament, it is proclaimed that God the Father will not let his children out of Hades until his first-born, Jesus, is willingly sacrificed, and descends into Hell to take their places. There the dead are eternally eaten, digested, and eaten again by Satan. In the images of Hell that decorate European cathedrals, inspired largely by Dante's *Divine Comedy*, Satan is always seen as a monster eating the damned, and his mouth is sometimes akin to the gates of Hell itself.

Hell

Furthermore, in the Grail legend, Parzival takes up the crown of the Fisher King after obtaining the kingdom's release from the spell caused by the Dolorous Stroke. Sometimes he is sent by the king to avenge his wounding by killing the rival king who hurt him. Then somehow the hero must use the very same sword or spear to cure the Fisher King's wound through sympathetic magic. In some versions, when this happens, the old man is finally able to die, and Parzival is revealed to be his nephew, who then takes his place as Grail king.

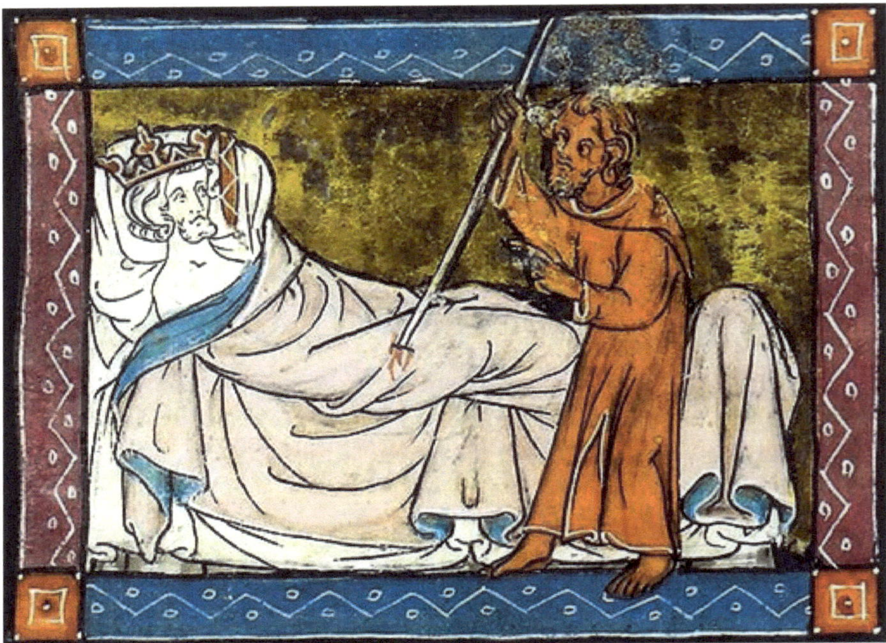

Another image of the Dolorous Stroke

Another story with this theme is that of Sleeping Beauty, who waits for a prince to discover her castle and kiss her, breaking the spell caused by pricking her finger on the cursed spindle. In older versions of this story, the hidden kingdom is called the Venusberg, and there the goddess of love waits for men to stumble upon her. When they do, she entraps them with a spell and makes them serve her for centuries as sex slaves.

This is exactly what the demon-witch Circe did to Odysseus in Homer's *Odyssey* when his ship landed on the shore of her land, drawn there by a magical attractive force. He was also held under a similar spell on the island of Calypso, and at one point his crewmembers had to stop their ears up with wax to prevent themselves from being drawn to their deaths by the irresistible call of the sirens (mermaids).

In his book *Aion: Researches Into the Phenomenology of the Self,* Carl Jung discussed the legendary "remora" or "echeneis." This was a fish to whom a magical magnetic property was ascribed by the sailors who reported encountering them. Supposedly, they exerted an invisible influence, so powerful that they could stop a ship dead in its tracks. As Jung explains:

> "The Echeneis exercises an attraction on ships that could best be compared with the influence of a magnet on iron. The attraction,

so the historical tradition says, emanates from the fish and brings the vessel, whether powered by sail or oarsmen, to a standstill. I mention this seemingly unimportant feature because ... in the alchemical view the attraction no longer proceeds from the fish but from a magnet which man possesses and which exerts the attraction that was once the mysterious property of the fish. If we bear in mind the significance of the fish, it is easy to understand why a powerful attraction should emanate from this arcane centre, which might aptly be compared with the magnetism of the North Pole..."

The Echeneis fish stopping a ship with its magnetic power

Jung says the fish of legend really represents the creative power of God sought by the alchemists, which they would imbibe, so as to internalize that power through digestion. Jung writes:

"What is it, then, that one adept whispers into the ear of another, fearfully looking round lest any betray them, or even guess their secret? Nothing less than this: that through this teaching the One and All, the Greatest in the guise of the Smallest, God himself in his everlasting fires, may be caught like a fish in the deep sea. Further, that he may be 'drawn from the deep' by a eucharistic act of integration (called teoqualo, 'Godeating,' by the Aztecs), and incorporated in the human body. This teaching

> is the secret and 'cunning' magnet by virtue of which the remora ('little in length, mighty in strength') [is caught] ..."

The "cunning magnet" is nothing less than the "Magnet of the Wise" or "Compass of the Wise," the "Philosophic Mercury" which the alchemists said could be used to extract the Philosopher's Stone from the lead of cosmic chaos, just as this magical fish could be overcome and drawn from the waters of the ocean. Of this, Jung says:

> "The 'magnet of the wise,' which is to draw the wonder-working fish to the surface can, our text says, be taught. The content of this secret teaching is the real arcanum of alchemy: the discovery or production of the prima materia. The 'doctrine' or 'theory' is personified or rather, concretized as 'Mercurius non vulgi,' the philosophical mercury. This conception is as ambiguous as the antique Hermes; sometimes Mercurius is a substance like quicksilver, sometimes it is a philosophy."

Jung went on to describe how this magnet or compass could be used to navigate the waters of chaos to the hidden kingdom at the center of the Earth, which can metaphorically be found, according to some legends, through a secret entrance at the North Pole. Quoting the alchemist Philathes, we read in *Aion* that:

> "... in the Pole is found the heart of Mercurius, 'which is the true fire wherein its Lord has his rest.
>
> He who journeys through this great and wide sea ... may guide his course by the sight of the North Star, which our Magnet will cause to appear unto you."

Then, Jung seems to be blown away by his own conception that the Lord of the Earth, interred in the Earth's center, is himself the source of that magnetic field, and the fire of Hades:

> "... I would emphasize, by way of recapitulation, that the infernal fire is nothing other than the Deus absconditus (hidden God) who dwells at the North Pole and reveals himself through magnetism. His other synonym is Mercurius, whose heart is to be found at the Pole, and who guides men on their perilous voyage over the sea of the world. The idea that the whole machinery of the world is driven by the infernal fire at the North Pole, that this is hell, and that hell is a system of upper powers reflected in the lower — this is a shattering thought."

This reference to the pole star as a guide to navigation can also be found in alchemy, where they say that the appearance of a six-pointed star heralds the birth of the alchemical "child." Jung again shares with a us a quote from Philathes that indicates the fate of this child once its location is determined with the help of the pole star or Compass of the Wise:

> "This, he says, is the 'ami minera' (the prima materia of the gold), 'the true key of our Work, without which no skill can kindle the fire of the lamp ... Do you, when you see his star, follow it to the cradle, and there you shall behold the fair infant. Cast aside your defilements, honour the royal child, open your treasure, offer a gift of gold; and after death he will give you 'flesh and blood, the supreme Medicine in the three monarchies of the earth ...'"

If it isn't already clear to you that this is a reference to the "wise men" — the alchemists — eating the flesh and blood of a child, Fulcanelli makes it even more obvious when addressing this same subject in *Mystery of the Cathedrals*:

> "... this sign has been called by the ancient authors the Seal of Hermes, Seal of the Wise (Sel des Sages, sel, salt, being put instead of Scel, seal, which confuses the mind of seekers), the Mark and the Imprint of the Almighty, his Signature, also the Star of the Magi, the Pole Star, etc. This geometric pattern remains and shows up more clearly when the gold to be dissolved is put into the mercury in order to restore it to its first state, that of young or rejuvenated gold, in other words to infant gold. That is why mercury — that faithful servant and Seal of the earth — is called the Fountain of Youth. The Philosophers are, therefore, speaking clearly when they teach that mercury, as soon as the solution has been carried out, bears the child, the Son of the Sun, the Little King (Kinglet), like a real mother, since the gold is indeed reborn in her womb. 'The wind — which is winged and volatile mercury — carried it in her belly', says Hermes in the Emerald Tablet. Furthermore, we find the secret version of this positive truth in the Epiphany cake, which it is the custom for families to eat at Epiphany, the famous feast marking the manifestation of the Christ Child to the three Magi-Kings and to the gentiles. Tradition has it that the Magi were guided to the cradle by a star, which was for them the annunciatory sign, the Good News of his birth. Our cake is signed like the matter itself and contains inside it the little child,

The appearance of the star, from Amiens cathedral, as presented by Fulcanelli

> commonly called the bather. It is the child Jesus, carried by Offerus, the servant or the traveller; it is the gold in its bath, the bather; it is the bean, the sabot, the cradle or the cross of honour and it is also the fish 'which swims in our philosophic water', according to the very expression of the Cosmopolite.'"

Of note there is an electrochemical effect called even by modern chemists the "Beating Heart of Mercury," which is produced when an iron nail touches a glob of liquid mercury. This causes the glob to pulse, and at times form the shape of a hexagram, the "Seal of Hermes." This effect would have been known to the alchemists of old.

Jung, like many other mythographers, saw the god of the Jewish religion as synonymous with Saturn, particularly because they celebrated their Sabbath, or "day of rest," on his holy day of Saturday (fitting since Saturn is the god of rest and leisure). Another connection between the Judaism and Saturn is the so-called "Star of David" or hexagram, which, Fulcanelli says, is also the "Hermetic seal" of the Great Work of the alchemists, the pole star that indicates the birth of the child destined to be ritually sacrificed (like Christ) and turned into gold. The hexagram and the number 6 are both associated with Saturn in ritual magic. That same can be said of the biblical God, who supposedly created the Earth in six days. Interestingly, the planet Saturn has a storm on its north pole as of this writing that is creating a bizarre electromagnetic effect taking the form of a hexagon as seen from space. The phenomenon has yet to be explained by scientists.

In 2007, a fascinating film about polar inter-dimensional portals and child sacrifice came out entitled *The Golden Compass*, based on a book called Northern Lights by Philip Pullman (part of a series called *His Dark Materials*). In this story, which takes place in a fantasy land, a scientist named Lord Asriel (like the alchemist warlock in The Smurfs) has discovered evidence of the existence of another dimension. This evidence involves the presence of a strange etheric substance called "Dust," visible at the North Pole. He believes that this substance is leaking in from the other dimension, and undertakes a journey to the Pole to find an entrance to this world.

An important part of the story is that, in the world in which it takes place, every single person is accompanied at every moment by a familiar spirit, literally called a "daemon," that takes the shape of an animal corresponding to their personality. With children, the daemon is able to shape-shift into different animal forms until the individual's core personality has solidified.

During this transition period, it is revealed that the children are vulnerable to "attack" from the pernicious influence of the Dust. The meaning of this is unclear, but is of great concern to the evil empire that rules this fictitious world, called the "Mysterium." They are believed by the main character, Asriel's niece Lyra, to be behind the theft of children that has been plaguing the orphanages and underclass families of the land. Lyra sets off on a quest to solve the mystery of these disappearing children, rumored to have been captured by enemies called "Gobblers."

To aid her in this quest, Lyra makes use of the "golden compass" referred to in the film's title, which is actually called an "alithiometer": a divination device for detecting truth. It looks like a large pocket watch, and contains wheels with strange emblems on them, which it uses to communicate oracles in answer to questions. In reply to these queries about the kidnappings, it points to images of a baby and a pot boiling over a fire.

The Alithiometer

Lyra later discovers that the children are being used in experiments in which they are permanently separated from their daemons, supposedly so that they can "grow up" properly. In fact, it drains them of vitality and ends up killing them. In the original book, it is revealed that Lord Asriel is in fact conducting similar experiments at the North Pole. It turns out that Lyra's whole quest has been a ruse all along, devised by him. His purpose was really to lure Lyra and her friend Roger to his polar laboratory. There, he separates the boy from his daemon and used the energy generated by this to power an inter-dimensional portal machine that he has invented. So instead of just looking for a portal, he created his own, ripping a giant hole in the atmosphere at the top of the Pole.

Shortcut to the castle, created by the Cheshire Cat

This story is rich on many levels, as are the other books in the series. The second part is called *The Subtle Knife*, which refers to a tool that can cut a window between dimensions (and can cut through anything else as well). This seems reminiscent of the Masonic and Arabian legends of the "shamir worm," which Hiram Abiff and/or Asmodeus purportedly used to cut the stones for Solomon's Temple. I think it may also be what Fulcanelli refers to in *Mystery of the Cathedrals* as "Le Bon Saber" ("the Good Sword"). It is the Flaming Sword, shaped like a lightning bolt, which cut a hole around paradise and created space-time, separating Adam and Eve from their home, who were trapped outside of the sacred boundary. It is the power by which the Cheshire Cat made a shortcut through the trunk of a tree and allowed Alice to go straight to the labyrinth that led to the castle of the Queen of Hearts. It is the Spear of Destiny which caused the wound of the Fisher King, and caused the kingdom to fall into a death-like trance, trapped in a bubble of chaos.

The location of the portal in Philip Pullman's novels indicates that the author has knowledge of the nineteenth and twentieth-century stories of secret entrances to a hidden underworld at the North and South poles, where supposedly could be found the so-called "Black Sun." This is a development of the more ancient concept of the hidden sun at the center of the Earth which is said to light the tomb of the sleeping god-king (or goddess-queen) of the fallen kingdom. In the ancient world, where some viewed the Earth as a flat disk, it was envisioned that the sun went to the Underworld at night, where it reigned as the "Midnight Sun," sometimes expressed in ancient artwork as a dark disk. The next morning it returned, reborn as the golden sun.

As the Earth moved through the cycle of the year, towards the Winter Solstice the sun spent more and more time "underground." Thus its death and rebirth was seen as happening on this larger scale as well, and was associated with the king-killing ritual of Saturnalia discussed in part 1 of this essay series (as well as in my book *Money Grows on the Tree of Knowledge*). In alchemy, this concept of the Black Sun or "Midnight Sun" was seen as synonymous with the "nigrido," the dead King Saturn, the "Chaos of the Wise" or prima materia that was the raw material for the Work. As Jung wrote in *Aion*:

> "Saturn, in astrology the 'star of the sun,' is alchemically interpreted as black; it is even called 'sol niger' and has a double nature as the arcane substance, being black outside like lead, but white inside."

The Black Sun is pure potential energy, the pre-elemental element that the Otherworld consists of, and of which our own world is made through reflection upon its shiny black surface. It is the blank slate or black mirror into which the magician or alchemist projects his consciousness. As it is reflected back to him, his perception of it creates the illusory reality he lives in. This is why mirrors, and other reflective surface, like lakes and baths, were seen as portals to the Otherworld, as demonstrated in Jewish folk legends of the kingdoms of Lilith and Asmodeus, and also repeatedly portrayed in the films of initiate Jean Cocteau. By staring into the Abyss, you can see and then experience new ways of organizing the particles of the universe to create new realities.

Alice traveling through the looking-glass into another world

In this way, the Black Sun corresponds to the power of the "Lord of the Earth," who, like Saturn, is said in myths to sleep in a hidden tomb at the center of the world, influencing surface reality with his dreams. Like Alice staring at the looking-glass, the creation of the Wonderland we live in occurs when Saturn sees his own projected image of his desired reality staring back at him from the Abyss, the dark mirror of the Black Sun. This is the meaning of the black orb seen in the palms of potentates the world over and from time immemorial. It is the "regnum in potentia" that they wield as their power, the word "potential" and "potentate" both being etymologically linked through the root word "potent," meaning "powerful and virile."

The word "reality," of course, is linked to "royalty" in European languages. Like a magic circle, the invisible political boundaries of a kingdom or "realm" dictate the confines within which everyone must live in the king's version of reality. It is through manipulation of the probabilities that govern the quantum world of possibilities that the priest-king manipulates reality. It is not what the king does that makes him powerful so much as what he can do. Once this potential energy becomes kinetic through action, the energy is spent, the hand is played, and the power is transferred elsewhere.

Not surprisingly, as the scientific era dawned and more was known about the cosmos, mystics began to adapt their metaphysics to the new physics, and new concepts were born to explain old symbols. The Black Sun came to be interpreted as being a dark sphere of energy that was literally present within the center of the Earth. It was thought to be the secret source of sustenance for a hidden kingdom called Agartha (no doubt linked to the kingdom of Asgarde in Norse mythology).

Some authors also wrote of the Black Sun as having influence upon the activities of the surface world, and some even thought of it as the source of the world's electromagnetic field. They believed that this subterranean kingdom could be accessed by secret entrances at the North and South poles, or through the caverns of the Himalayas. Supposedly, certain secret societies were in contact with "hidden masters" from Agartha, who conspired with them on how to control the populations of the Earth.

Numerous science fiction authors and mystical adepts wrote about concepts like Agartha and the Black Sun from the nineteenth century to the mid-twentieth, including Jules Verne, H.G. Wells, H.P. Lovecraft, H.P. Blavatsky, and Alexandre Saint-Yves d'Alveydre. It was the latter author who wrote about the politics of the hidden kingdom. He purported that a political system existed called "synarchy," which involved a surface world (ours) governed by a wise council of elders (the secret chiefs or illuminati, drawn from the world's secret societies), who were themselves governed by hidden masters from the inner world below the Earth's surface.

Strangely, these ideas of a Black Sun and an underground kingdom did have a direct influence on politics during World War II, as it appears that leaders on both sides believed in such notions. On the Nazi side, Himmler and perhaps even the Fuhrer himself were converts to the concepts. To Himmler, the Grail stone and the Black Sun were the same thing, and he purchased a castle in the German village of Wewelsburg, where he planned to build a modern "Grail castle" for special work with elite members of his S.S. ("Schutzstaffel" or "Protection Squadron") military corps.

On the floor of the lowest chamber in the building, Himmler created an "inner sanctum" where rituals would be performed, and on the floor he placed the symbol of the Black Sun that was being employed by contemporary German mystical orders: a wheel, the hub of which radiated lightning-bolt-shaped rays. The German orders saw the swastika as the original root symbol representing this concept, and its use may have signified, to the inner hierarchy of the Reich, a shorthand code for the secret source of their government's power.

The Black Sun symbol at Wewelsburg Castle

The Spear of Destiny, believed to have pieced the side of Christ (or the Fisher King)

The Nazi government sponsored all sorts of bizarre missions to search for magical artifacts, including the Holy Grail, the Spear of Destiny, and the Ark of the Covenant. Other missions purportedly included a trip to Antarctica to search for an entrance to the inner Earth, and another one to the Himalayas for the same purpose (among others). Many members of the inner hierarchy of Hitler's administration had been influenced by a secret mystical order called the Vril Society. This group believed that Germans were of the "Aryan" race, descended, they believed, from a superhuman species that lived in the center of the Earth. They believed that this underground race used the "light of the Black Sun," the so-called "Vril force" or "Green Ray," as the power source for an advanced technology.

Insignia of the S.S. with death's head and lightning bolts (sig runes)

These mystics were into channeling, and believed that they were in contact with these hidden chiefs of the inner world. Purportedly, information was passed on about how to use the energy of the Black Sun to build anti-gravity craft and time machines. Allegedly, the Germans later developed flying saucers based on this technology (called "foo fighters" by the Allied pilots who witnessed them in the war theater). They are also said to have built a machine called "the Bell" that may have been meant to act as a time machine or inter-dimensional portal. The use of the lightning-bolt shaped sign rune as the logo for the S.S., along with the Death's Head (symbol of the alchemical nigrido) may have been intended as a reference to the natural force of electromagnetism that many mystics thought was the very real manifestation of the Black Sun's power.

One the side of the Allies in World War II, a Russian mystic named Nicholas Roerich was heavily influential on the US administration. President Roosevelt and his Secretary of Agriculture, Henry Wallace, as well as his Treasury Secretary, Henry Morgenthau, were all members of the same Masonic lodge. Through Wallace they all came to be persuaded by Roerich, who believed that he was in contact with the hidden masters of Agartha. He convinced Wallace to arrange government financing for a quest for the "foundation stone of the world," which he believed to be in the Himalayas. Under the guise of a trip to obtain agricultural samples, the adventure was embarked upon, at American taxpayer expense.

The whole incident later became a major embarrassment for the administration. Nonetheless, there is no reason to think that belief in such things was not still rampant in the upper echelons of the government. After the war, Nazi scientists who had worked on secret projects with purportedly Agarthan technology were smuggled into the US and recruited to work for NASA as part of a CIA operation called "Project Paperclip."

At this point in our study we really must mention the work of David Talbot, who is building upon theories of Immanuel Velikovsky regarding major cosmic cataclysm in our solar system in the distant past. Talbot speculates that during the antediluvian Golden Age, when the Earth's tilt was much different, Saturn was the dominant orb in the night's sky. He believes that most of the symbols said by mythographers to represent the sun are in fact depicting Saturn, and that it was *his* chariot or boat in the night's sky whose movements the priests of the ancient world were really concerned with. This is because, he says, everything back then looked much different than it does now.

The Earth's magnetic field, in addition to protecting us from the damaging effects of solar radiation, also creates a boundary that prevents us from seeing what would otherwise be fantastic optical effects in the sky, caused by that very radiation. At the North and South poles these effects can be seen even today as a colorful aurora. Talbot believes that in the past, when the magnetic field was much weaker (as it always is before and after a major shift of the poles), Saturn formed a spectacular sight in the arch of the sky, as did the other heavenly bodies.

When at times their images conjoined at times, they formed what Talbot calls the "polar configuration": an image that was represented by ancient man as a starburst or a cross. Talbot has made computer simulations of all the different forms these shapes might have taken in the sky as the Earth's axis continued to shift, and the magnetic field varied in intensity. He believes that these shapes formed the origins for a great many of the most common religious symbols used in the ancient world. He also used these simulations to interpret all of the earliest myths as describing the movements of this configuration in interaction with other heavenly bodies, as seen from Earth by our supposedly primitive ancestors.

A hair-raising fact to consider is that scientists acknowledge that the Earth's magnetic field has been getting much weaker in the last couple of hundred years, and is weakening at an exponentially increasing rate that is now advancing quite rapidly. Perhaps this explains some of the bizarre optical effects in the sky that have been seen by observers in the last couple of years. These include the image of a twin sun at dawn and dusk, sightings of which have been reported dozens of times. Also, dozens of spiral-shaped light formations have been seen over the same time period, with a dark hole in the center, making the appearance of a vortex or portal. Traditional flying saucer-type UFOs have even been recorded vanishing into these holes. In addition, images that look remarkably like the old German Black Sun symbol have appeared mysteriously on the radar at an Australian weather station.

Talbot is part of a minority in the scientific community who hold to alternative theories involving the properties of plasma, the so-called "fourth state of matter." Plasma is said even by mainstream science to be the true fundamental state of all matter, a real alchemical "prima materia." Without going into detail beyond the scope of this essay, let us say that Talbot and his colleagues believe that plasma which we cannot see is creating electromagnetic energy throughout the universe that is currently going unnoticed. They think that this is the true source of the gravitational effects measured in space, which have traditionally been attributed by scientists to invisible "dark matter."

In this alternative viewpoint, these scientists turn on its head Einstein's Theory of Relativity, which is based upon a definition of gravity that Einstein himself acknowledged was flawed. Instead of matter, they say it is the electromagnetism of the hidden plasma that is "bending space-time." This, then, would be a viable description of the power of the Black Sun, and would raise it from merely a power within the center of the Earth to a wholly universal phenomenon. It would also explain why the Black Sun's "rays" were thought by German mystics to be useful for creating antigravity, as well as their obsession with lightning bolts.

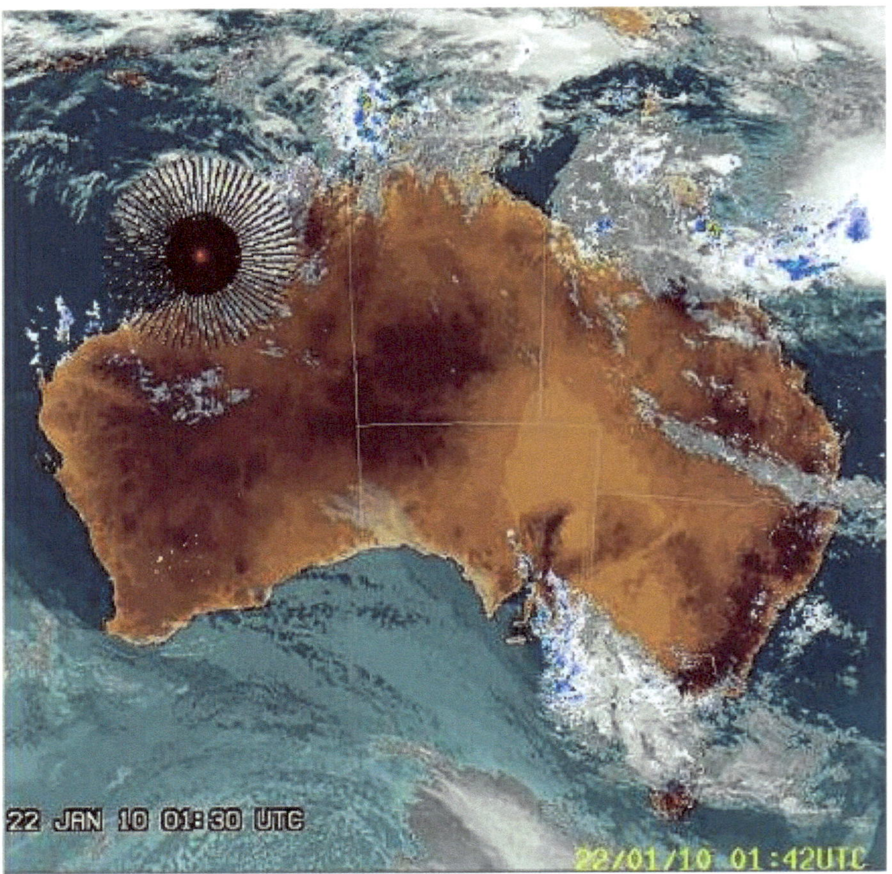

An image resembling the Black Sun, from the radar of an Australian weather monitoring station

This is also the basis of some alternative theories about what exactly powers the heat of the sun (presently thought to be nuclear explosions taking place within its core). These theories connect with modern experiments dealing with a technology derisively called "cold fusion" by its critics. Trend forecaster Gerald Celente recently proclaimed that this would be the basis of a new alternative energy source that could have a "game-changing" effect on geopolitics. Interestingly, cold fusion has always been openly compared to alchemy by both its critics and its devotees.

Talbot has many detailed theories about how plasma may have caused electromagnetic bolts to form between heavenly bodies, with cataclysmic effects upon every planet in the solar system. He believes that this happened at least once, and perhaps several times, in the distant past, and that it may happen again someday, as part of a cyclical cosmic pattern. His documentary film *Thunderbolts of the Gods* is a fascinating exploration of these theories.

The idea that we are living in a universe powered by an unseen source of electromagnetic energy, forming an invisible web around us, governing the movements of the heavens, can only increase the paranoid feeling that this really is like *The Matrix.* It truly does seem like a giant machine being run for the benefit of someone either too large to see, or just outside of our perception in another dimension. Perhaps we are unable to see that "someone" because the machine is part of its internal organs, within which we may very well be being digested slowly without ever knowing it. But what would our jail-masters' aim truly be for keeping us in a clockwork such as this?

A Grail knight with the Black Sun on his shield

That is something which we shall explore in future installments of this essay. But in the meantime it is interesting to note that the Earth's core is believed by mainstream scientists to be made of iron, and this is thought to be the real source of the Earth's electromagnetic field. Many alchemical texts referred not to the transmutation of lead so much as that of iron. I suppose that would make the iron core the real "Black Sun," which really is beginning to exert its powerful influence upon the surface of the Earth, in the form of magnetic pole shifts, earthquakes, and volcanic eruptions.

Once again, let us recall that the Romans and the Indians both believed that the Kali Yuga, the last aeon before the rebirth of the Golden Age, would be the "Iron Age." They said it would be ruled by a war-like race made of iron, the metal thought by alchemists to correspond to Mars, the god of war. They would ravage the Earth with violence before being unmercifully snuffed out by the great alchemist in the sky, anxious to throw the Earth into a cosmic athanor, so that it may be reborn again pure and new like gold. Only the elect — those who known how to cut a hole in the cosmos and build an ark made of space-time — will survive the coming cataclysm.

Part III: Hero’s Journey to Hell

Part III: Hero's Journey to Hell

Former UFO Peggy Kane has a message for humanity: the gods just want to rape you and eat you. This is the rather sobering conclusion she has come to after countless hours of analyzing messages from beyond this earthly plane via EVP (electronic voice phenomenon) divination sessions. Anyone who has seen an episode of a modern ghost-hunting reality show knows that "EVPs" are messages that can be heard on either a digital or analog tape sound recording. People will record themselves talking to disembodied spirits and then play the recording back to hear the spirit's reply, usually whispered and faint, as well as distorted-sounding.

Peggy Kane began doing this many years ago after a long career as a UFO expert. She used it as a way to contact extraterrestrial intelligences that allegedly resided in parallel dimensions. But then she decided to go a step forward. She applied a technique known "reverse speech analysis," perfected by David John Oates. Allegedly, if you reverse a recording of someone talking, it will say something else that will reveal what the person was really thinking as he or she was speaking. If the message is congruent, they were being honest at the time. But frequently the perceived backwards message is something at variance with the initial message and allegedly reveals the truth that the speaker wishes to remain secret.

When Peggy Kane applied this technique to the ET EVPs she was recording, it painted a picture of reality that was totally different from what we perceive on the surface. It was a much more sinister view of our world, as well as the world beyond, and what happens to us when we die.

UFO expert Linda Molton Howell once posited: "Could it be that death is the ultimate UFO abduction experience?" That is the conclusion that Peggy Kane has come to, and the intentions of our abductors are not nice at all, according to her.

Peggy says that our reality is being controlled from outside forces that do not have our best interests in mind. They are using both our bodies and souls for food, amusement, and scientific experimentation. Their world is what we consider to be the "astral realm" from our perspective over here. But when we leave our bodies to travel over there (which, she says, we do frequently), then it is perceived as a physical world just like our own. There are buildings, streets, factories, stores, and money being exchanged over there just like there is here. But the universe on the other side is ruled by a bloodthirsty race of Reptilians. The walk upright like humans. But that is where the similarity ends.

According to Peggy, the Reptilians keep humans in a 3rd-dimensional prison by the use of some sort of artificial force field called "the Net." The situation is very similar to how the human slaves in the film The Matrix were kept by their robot overlords in little capsules floating in goo. There they were used as batteries and bled of their energy while they lived their lives in a computer-generated dream-world. While in this artificial prison, Peggy says that we are constantly being drained of both our physical and astral energy by our hidden masters. They are constantly sucking our soul energy, as well as our blood and other body fluids, and we are unaware of it. The soul energy is called "Loosh," allegedly, and pre-adolescent children are the best source.

In order to feed off of us, Ms. Kane says the Reptilians sometimes possess our bodies, the way we think of demon possession. This is called "being seeded," according to Peggy. They open portals or "mind gates" into the human psyche that allow them to whisper suggestions that result in altering the possessed person's behavior according to the parasite's wishes. This can then create whatever emotional response the parasite wishes to feed off of. If the Reptilian inside you really enjoys the emotions you give off when you are fighting with your boyfriend, then he will whisper suggestions to you that instigate these situations.

They also make direct use of your "astral body" on the other side, according to Peggy. As soon as people die, and their spirit travels to the other side, they are eaten, just like the worst sinners are depicted being eaten by the Devil in Dante's Inferno. Peggy says that this is taking place even on supposedly "dead" planets in our own solar system. Ms. Kane says that Mars is a central hub for the trafficking of "astral body parts."

But that's perhaps not the worst of it. According to Peggy, the Reptilians make use of us sexually as well. "Reptilians pull people out of their bodies at night and rape them," she says. "They do it to almost everybody," both male and female. The purpose of this, she believes, is that it is another way of stealing our energy. "Rape is one of the ways they feed," says Peggy. "They call that 'alien honey.'"

Another reason for this rape is breeding, for according to Peggy, there are no new births on the other side. The babies are allegedly often taken by the Reptilians before they are born. At one point, she says, they made her pregnant and then pulled the fetus out in the middle of the night, leaving her in extreme physical pain. Some of these babies are eaten right away on the other side, and others are raised to be slaves of various sorts before being eventually eaten upon their astral death at the end.

Peggy says that many of the Reptilians delight in toying with psychics and channelers who attempt to contact the spiritual dimension. They play the roles of gods, guardian angels, familiar spirits, departed relatives, and whatever else the seeking person wishes to see. They set up situations where the people they contact agree to give them even more "loosh," along with blood sacrifices, opportunities to possess human bodies, and sexual favors. However, this activity is also thought to be dangerous by the Reptilians in charge on the other side, so they try to restrict it. According to Peggy, "It's illegal over there now to talk into a recorder."

Peggy Kane appears to view all religions, cults, and spiritual movements as the result of such fraudulent contacts and seems to agree with my own assessment, which I have written about in several previous books (including *Solomon's Treasure* and *Hocus Pocus*), describing such institutions as "spiritual pyramid schemes" for the benefit of the spiritual entities at the top. The "near-death experience is a ruse," says Peggy. After our bodies are raped and eaten on the other side. She says they are brought back to Earth again for another round of life. According to Ms. Kane, reincarnation exists to keep us in "the game."

Many will recognize Peggy Kane's stories as having influenced the work of David Icke, who has posited that the world is run by multidimensional Reptoids who can shapeshift into human form. They do this, he says, by projecting a sort of hologram over their Reptilian skin. Icke believes that most of the powerful people on this Earth are actually Reptilians. He says that they can be traced back to certain aristocratic families that have ruled the Earth and interbred with one another since the beginnings of recorded history. Icke says that they belong to secret societies that worship Satan (as well as a host of pagan deities). They are involved in the widespread kidnapping, rape, and eating of people, especially children, which are all forms of sustenance that they need. Without blood and rape the Reptoids would not have the strength to hold their humanoid form, according to Icke.

This, of course, matches up in many ways with my own research. In my book *The Merovingian Mythos*, I trace the origins of both the religious traditions of Europe and the royal families of Europe to the alleged bloodline of Cain, which supposedly descended directly from the "serpent" in the Garden of Eden. I showed how ancient legends described these original god-kings as actually ruling on Earth directly, interbreeding with humans and ruling over them, until eventually the admixture of human and divine blood became so diluted that they now look like normal humans. I also wrote about the clues indicating that their serpent ancestors were trapped in a spiritual prison in the center of the Earth because of their crimes against God (among them, raping and eating humans). There they await eventual release by their human-hybrid descendants.

I furthermore quoted the work of one Nicholas de Vere, who writes about these royal bloodlines as ultimately descending from the "Dragon race" (from the Serpent of Eden). He claims to be a scion of one of their royal orders, the Dragon Court, and says that they have magical powers, belong to secret societies that conduct Satanic rituals (since Satan is their literal ancestor), retain their magical potency by drinking blood (particularly menstrual blood), and are sexually aggressive by nature. De Vere and his (now late) former research partner Laurence Gardner have been accused by David Icke of being shapeshifting reptiles themselves.

All of this stuff about shapeshifting reptiles from parallel dimensions has been nothing but an amusing urban legend to me for many years. But recent research into ancient mythology has caused me to reassess. Due to my discovery of certain patterns within these old myths, I am now inclined to believe that mankind has for some time been aware that his gods are feeding upon him in the otherworld, and have chosen to represent them in the form of bloodsucking reptiles.

Joseph Campbell was known for his brilliant analysis of universal themes in world mythology, which he wrote about in his *book The Hero With a Thousand Faces*. What Campbell was saying was not that every single myth tells the same story, but that there is one grand story, one "Monomyth" of which they are all a part, transcending and unifying them all. Like the tapestry woven by Penelope in Homer's *Odyssey*, the story of the Monomyth can never be finished. For if it were ever completed, that would mean that the sacred king, the hero of the Monomyth, would have to be officially declared dead, lost in the Abyss, and all hope for the redemption of the kingdom would be gone.

So just as any individual novel, short story, or film might be part of a larger series, or the characters might all occupy the same fictional world as those of other, related works, the stories that our ancestors passed on through the generations are all part of the same Master Epic. However, because it takes place in a nonlocal Otherworld beyond time and space, each act of the play can have infinite variations in action and outcome, including the very identity of the characters involved and the alignment of their relationships to one another. In any given story you may either witness the journey to the Otherworld, and the return as well (the classic Hero's Journey). Then again, you may only get to see the departure, or the return, outside of the context of the rest of the story. Or you may only get a fragment a story taking place within another dimension, without any backstory as to how the characters got into the Otherworld in the first place (as in the classic fairy tale that begins "Once upon a time …")

But what does the Hero's Journey actually mean? It has been interpreted as a form of initiation and soul transformation, like a coming-of-age morality tale, wherein one learns a lesson about personal growth and maturity. It can certainly be that if you want to see it that way. However, I am here to offer a more sinister interpretation, from the point of view of the person doing the initiating. Joseph Campbell said that the hero is always "called" to his adventure. He might well have considered who it is that is doing the calling, and under what motivation.

As I have established in earlier installments of this essay series, there is a theme in various myths of an initiator (Chronos, Venus, the Fisher King, etc) luring the main character of a story into his or her realm in the Otherworld. It is often presented as a chance for the hero to obtain a magical power of some sort, usually represented as either an artifact (a holy cup, lance, or stone) or a sacred substance (ambrosia, soma, nectar, or the alchemical elixir). Sometimes he sets off to save a woman who has been abducted by a god or demon for sexual purposes. Sometimes in the course of his journey he also finds himself being used for sex by a goddess or demoness.

The thesis I wish to put forward is that, in our most archetypal stories (from old folklore and mythology to fairy tales, and even modern TV show, films and novels), human beings tend to tell tales of adventures into another dimension, which seems conceptually to be one and the same with the realm of the dead, the astral realm, and the dreamy realm of sleep. But in each of these stories, the hero or heroine is in fact being enticed to sacrifice his or her life, including blood, flesh, and soul, to the inhabitants of the Otherworld (be they gods, demons, vampires, giants, or whatever). Their need to feast on these things is based on the fact that they have no life in themselves, so thus they have no blood, and no souls. This is not always overtly stated in the story, but is nonetheless frequently implied.

Sometimes the soul of the sacrificed is replaced by that of someone in the Otherworld, with the implication that this sacrifice is necessary so that someone in the Otherworld can experience life again. Sometimes it seems that a god or demon of the Otherworld is trying to possess the body of a living human through sexual union, either to inhabit the body of the lover, or to be incarnated through the child that is conceived by the union. Sometimes, quite frequently, there is a story element involving a child that is sacrificed so that the reign of the king or queen of the Otherworld can continue. Often the child sacrificed is the heir of the monarch, or someone else's child is sacrificed as a substitute for the monarch's son. Sometimes the hero or heroine is lured onto the adventure to rescue this child from certain death.

If the hero of the story is in fact a heroine, quite often she if overtly abducted and taken to the Otherworld, although she may be lured to a spot where she can be easily taken. This is the story of Persephone taken by Hades for his wife. Although this is referred to as the "rape" of Persephone, the word "rape" is related to "rapture" and meant "to be taken away" for the purposes of sex or marriage. Originally the word had nothing to do with the consent, or lack thereof, on the part of the female. The word later took on the meaning of "elicit sexual union" and generally referred to forbidden marriages between particular tribes (as the term is frequently used in the Bible). What it really referred to originally is a marriage between a mortal and a being from the other side.

The purpose of the hero or heroine being abducted or lured to the Otherworld is very sinister indeed. It really represents a person's soul or astral body being projected from their physical body. Once this is done, the soul can become food for those on the other side, while the still animate body can be used as a vehicle for those spirits wishing to incarnate into the physical realm. The reason why the hero's journey typically ends with "apotheosis," the hero dying to his humanity and being reborn as an immortal, is because this is exactly what is being represented. The hero's soul has disappeared into the Abyss and been replaced with that of an "immortal" from the Otherworld.

[In my forthcoming book, *The Portalnaut's Guide to the Otherworld*, I will explain the details of this new interpretation of the Hero's Journey, and what it means for us all.] **END**

Published by Tracy R. Twyman as a three part series in quintessentialpublications.com (2011)

www.ingramcontent.com/pod-product-compliance
Lightning Source LLC
Chambersburg PA
CBHW041926180726
48295CB00003B/87